OUR LADY

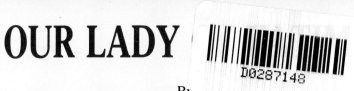

By

REV. LAWRENCE G. LOVASIK, S.V.D.
Divine Word Missionary

NIHIL OBSTAT: Daniel V. Flynn, J.C.D., *Censor Librorum*
IMPRIMATUR: ✠ James P. Mahoney, D.D., *Vicar General, Archdiocese of New York*
© 1984 *by Catholic Book Publishing Corp.*, N.Y. — Printed in Hong Kong

ISBN 978-0-89942-387-6   www.catholicbookpublishing.com
CPSIA   June 2013   10 9 8 7 6 5 4 3   A/P

An Angel Appears to Three Children

IN the Spring of 1916, an angel appeared to three children tending sheep in a pasture in the village of Fatima, Portugal. The older girl, Lucia Santos, was nine, and her two cousins Francisco and Jacinta Marto were eight and six. The angel taught them special prayers and told them that he was the Angel of Peace, the Guardian Angel of Portugal.

The angel taught them to say: "My God, I believe, I adore, I hope, and I love You. I ask forgiveness for those who do not believe, nor hope, nor love You."

The angel asked them to pray for sinners and for peace, and to bear the suffering the Lord would send them.

The next year Sunday, May 13, 1917, the children were with their flock of sheep in a field called the Cova. They said the rosary after lunch and then they played. They were frightened by two flashes of lightning out of the clear sky.

The children said an angel gave them Communion. 3

The children saw a beautiful young woman.

A Beautiful Lady Appears

THE children saw a beautiful young woman standing over a small oak tree surrounded by a bright light. Her clothing was pure white, and a mantle edged with gold covered her head and flowed around her body. A gold cord ending in a tassel hung around her neck. Her hands were joined, and from her right arm hung a white rosary of pearly beads.

With a smile of motherly tenderness, but somewhat sad, she told the children to come near, saying, "Have no fear, I will do you no harm. I come from heaven. I want you children to come here on the thirteenth of each month, until October. Then I will tell you who I am."

"Do you come from heaven? Will I go there?" asked Lucia.

"Yes," replied the Lady, "but you must say the rosary, and say it devoutly."

After the vision the children returned to their homes.

The Children Tell Their Secret

AT supper that evening, Jacinta told her mother what had happened, but she did not believe her story. Her brothers and sisters— all home for Sunday night supper—spread the story throughout the village the next day. Relatives and friends gathered in their home demanding to know why the children were telling such lies.

Lucia's mother was angry with her when she told her secret. Within twenty-four hours after the children had seen the Lady the prediction she had made— "You will have much to suffer"—started coming true.

Only the father of Jacinta and Francisco believed the things that were happening at Fatima. He did not think that his children would lie to him. The priest said to him: "Let the children go to the Cove. Then bring them to me and I'll question them one by one."

When the people heard about the story, they made fun of the children. They thought that they were lying.

Lucia's mother was angry when Lucia told her secret.

7

8   The Lady asked the children to say the Rosary.

The Lady Comes Again

THE Lady's second visit happened on June 13. The children knelt down near the oak tree and began to say the rosary. A flash of lightning came from the clear sky. Lucia cried out: "Our Lady is coming."

The Lady appeared in a bright light and asked the children to say the rosary every day and to say after each mystery: "O Jesus, forgive us our sins, save us from the fire of hell. Take all souls to heaven, and especially those most in need of Your mercy."

Lucia asked the Lady if she would take the children to heaven. She said: "Francisco and Jacinta soon, but you must remain on earth to spread the devotion to my Immaculate Heart."

On July 13, 5000 people were present when the children came to the Cova with their flocks. The Lady appeared for the third time.

The Virgin Mary foretold the Second World War and the coming of Communism. She asked for the consecration of Russia to her Immaculate Heart.

The Promise of a Miracle

ON August 13, the mayor of the town came in his carriage and took the children away as they were leaving for the Cova. After asking them many questions, he put them in jail. He tried to make them change their story. Since they would not do so, they were released from the jail.

Although the children were not at the Cova, over 15,000 people were on hand and said the rosary. At noon there was a flash of lightning and a clap of thunder; then a glowing cloud settled over the little tree where the Lady usually appeared.

On September 13, more than 30,000 people gathered at the Cova. The Lady appeared again and asked the children to pray for peace.

Lucia asked for a miracle that would prove what the children had seen. The Lady promised a miracle that would happen on October 13.

During the vision, the whole crowd saw a shower of white petals fall from the sky, only to melt a few inches from the ground.

The mayor asked the children many questions.   11

12   **The children knelt in the mud and prayed.**

The Lady of the Rosary

ON the morning of October 13, when the children arrived at the Cova, 70,000 people filled the field hoping to see the Lady. But they never did.

Rain began to fall heavily. At noon the three children knelt down in the mud to pray the rosary. A sharp flash of lightning stilled the great crowd. A dim cloud rested on the oak tree.

The beautiful Lady appeared in radiant brightness. Lucia asked the question: "Who are you and what do you want?"

The Lady said: "I am the Lady of the Rosary, and I have come to warn the faithful to amend their lives and ask pardon for their sins. People must not continue to offend the Lord, Who is already so deeply offended. They must say the rosary."

The Virgin Mary then asked that a church be built on the spot and promised the war would end in a year if people would amend their lives.

Francisco made his First Communion on his deathbed.

16

The Deaths of Francisco and Jacinta

ON April 4, 1919, Francisco died of influenza, making his First Communion on his death-bed. He had been faithful to the wishes of the Blessed Virgin and had said many rosaries each day and made sacrifices to make up for the sins of people since the first vision.

Jacinta also became ill, and the Blessed Mother appeared to her a number of times. She, too, was faithful to the requests of Our Lady of Fatima and died in a Lisbon hospital on February 20, 1920.

When her body was taken out of the grave September 13, 1935, it was found to be incorrupt.

The cause for the beatification of Francisco and Jacinta has begun. Both children are buried in the large basilica of Our Lady of Fatima, Francisco on the right and Jacinta in the left transept.

Lucia in a Convent

LUCIA, whom the Blessed Mother made her messenger and on whom she placed the burden of making known her wishes, left Fatima in 1921 and worked in an orphanage.

Lucia ever remained faithful in carrying out the wishes of the Blessed Virgin Mary. She knew that Our Lady of Fatima wanted her to live a life of holiness to be an example to the whole world of the spirit of the message given her by Mary.

In 1925 she entered the Convent of the Sisters of St. Dorothy and received the name of Sister Mary Lucia of Sorrows. In 1948 she became a Carmelite nun.

Lucia was asked by her spiritual director to put into writing certain graces that she had received. Our Lord made known to her that she should now make known what the Blessed Mother had told her about devotion to her Immaculate Heart.

Lucia became a nun. 19

Devotion to Our Lady Approved

THE close of the First World War and the rise of Communism had proved that what the Blessed Virgin foretold was really true.

In 1930 the bishop of Leira declared the apparitions to the three children at Fatima as worthy of belief. 215 cures took place in the 13 years since the Virgin Mary appeared.

Pope Pius XII approved the devotion to Our Lady of Fatima and consecrated the world to her Immaculate Heart, October 31, 1943.

In 1945 Pope Pius XII approved the feast of the Immaculate Heart of Mary to promote this devotion for the peace of the world. He also consecrated Russia to her Immaculate Heart.

Pope Paul VI, in the Vatican Council, again consecrated the world to the Immaculate Heart of Mary on November 21, 1969.

Pope John Paul II visited Fatima and urged all Catholics to say the Rosary each day.

Pope Pius XII approved devotion to Our Lady of Fatima. 21

The Basilica at Fatima

TODAY there is a large basilica at the place where the Virgin Mary appeared to which hundreds of thousands of pilgrims come from all over the world each year.

There Holy Masses are offered and Holy Communion given, confessions are heard and people say the rosary.

From May 13 to October 13 special pilgrimages and devotions are held at the Basilica. A crowd of more than 200,000 people fill the large area called the esplanade, in front of the Basilica.

In the middle of the esplanade is a high pillar on which stands the Sacred Heart. A small wooden chapel in the esplanade with the statue of Our Lady of Fatima marks the place where Mary appeared.

The large golden statue of the Sacred Heart of Jesus in the middle of the esplanade reminds all the pilgrims that Mary's mission is to lead us to her Son.

Special devotions are held at the Basilica. 23

Through Mary to Jesus

WE owe special veneration by word and example to Mary as Mother of Christ, Mother of the Church, and our spiritual Mother. In doing this we imitate her Son Who loved and honored His Mother more than any other human being that ever lived.

Jesus made His Mother holier and more beautiful than any other member of His Church, for she is truly the Mother of the Church.

Some of the special gifts Mary received from God are: being Mother of God, being preserved from all stain of original sin, and being taken body and soul to heaven.

By honoring the Mother of Jesus we show our love for her Son, who made her so holy and beautiful. He made her so powerful as Queen of Heaven that she may help us, her children, in all our needs.

Through her prayers we can receive the grace we need to be more like Jesus and to save our souls. By following her example and by seeking her help in prayer we can be sure of reaching her Son in eternal life.

In honoring Mary, we imitate her Son.

The apparitions at Fatima call to mind Mary as Queen of heaven and her interest in the salvation of mankind on earth. Through the rosary and penance she brings blessings upon her needy children. She appeals for peace in the world.

Our Lady asked
for devotion to
her Immaculate Heart.

The Immaculate Heart of Mary

OUR Lady told the children at Fatima that her heart is the hope of the world. In a vision to Sister Mary Lucia, she asked for the spread of devotion to her Immaculate Heart: "To save souls God wishes to establish in the world the devotion to my Immaculate Heart." She also appealed for the daily rosary.

She promised: "If people do what I tell you, many souls will be saved and there will be peace."

"I come to ask the consecration of Russia to my Immaculate Heart and I ask that the Communion of Reparation be made in atonement for the sins of the world on the five first Saturdays of every month. Please say the rosary."

The Virgin Mary promised: "If my wishes are fulfilled, Russia will be converted, and there will be peace; if not, then Russia will spread her errors throughout the world, bringing new wars and persecutions of the Church; the good will be martyred, and the Holy Father will have much to suffer. But in the end, my Immaculate Heart will triumph."

We should answer our Lady's requests by a great love for her Son in the Holy Eucharist at Holy Mass and Holy Communion. We should consecrate ourselves to her Immaculate Heart and pray the rosary that God may forgive sinners and grant peace to the world.

If we do what our Blessed Mother asks, we can be sure of coming closer to Jesus and reaching eternal life in heaven.

Prayer to the Immaculate Heart of Mary

MARY, Virgin Mother of God and our Mother, at Fatima you asked us to honor your Immaculate Heart. In honoring your Immaculate Heart we honor your person and the love you have for us.

The heavenly Father prepared you, Virgin Mary, to be the worthy Mother of His Son. He let you share beforehand in the salvation Christ would bring by His death, and kept you sinless from the first moment of your conception. Help us by your prayers to live in His presence without sin.

Almighty God gave you, a humble virgin, the privilege of being the Mother of His Son, and crowned you with the glory of heaven. May your prayers bring us to the salvation of Christ and raise us up to eternal life.

You stood beneath the cross when your Son entrusted us to your care and made you our Mother also. We, your children, turn to you with confidence.

Our Lady of Fatima, pray for us.

The heavenly Father raised you, the sinless Virgin, Mother of His Son, body and soul to the glory of heaven. May we see heaven as our final goal and come to share your glory. May we follow your example in reflecting your holiness in our life and join in your hymn of endless joy and praise in heaven.

Prayer to Mary, Queen of Peace

MARY, Virgin Mother of God and Queen of Heaven, your loving Son Jesus has offered Himself as a perfect sacrifice for all mankind to reconcile us with His Father and to bring us the peace of the children of God. Help us to seek God and live in His love that we may enjoy true peace.

Ask your Son Jesus, Who gives us the peace that is not of this world and Who has washed away our hatred with His blood, to banish the violence and evil of sin and keep us safe from weapons of hate. Help us to overcome war and violence, and to establish God's law of love and justice.

May those who are at peace with one another keep the goodwill that unites them; may those who are enemies forget their hatred and be healed through the Blood of Your Son.

Mary, Queen of Peace, bring peace to the world.

Our Lady of Fatima, Queen of Peace, may we always profit by your prayers, for you bring us life and salvation through Jesus Christ your Son. Hear our prayer and give us peace in our time that we may rejoice in God's mercy and praise Him without end.

Prayer to Our Lady of Fatima

OUR Lady of the Rosary, ask your Son Jesus to have mercy on us and to give us His peace. Help us to heed your warning at Fatima that we amend our lives and stop hurting God, Who is already so deeply offended by our sins.

Our Lady of Fatima, Queen of the Holy Rosary, pray for us.